Farm Animals

Sheep

Rachael Bell

Heinemann Library
Chicago, Illinois

Customer Service 888-454-2279

Designed by AMR
Originated by Ambassador Litho
Printed in Hong Kong/China

04 03 02
10 9 8 7 6 5 4 3

Library of Congress Cataloging-in-Publication Data
Bell, Rachael.
    Sheep / Rachael Bell.
        p. cm. – (Farm animals)
    Includes bibliographical references and index.
    Summary: Introduces this familiar farm animal by describing its physical appearance, manner of reproduction, eating, and sleeping habits, ways of staying healthy, required care, and uses.
    ISBN 1-57572-533-9
    1. Sheep-- Juvenile literature. 2. [1. Sheep.] I. Title.
SF 375.2B46 2000
636.3--dc21   99-043370
                                                  CIP

Acknowledgments
The Publishers would like to thank the following for permission to reproduce photographs: Agripicture/Peter Dean, p. 21; J. Allan Cash Ltd., p. 27; Anthony Blake Photo Library/Sue Atkinson, p. 23; Bruce Coleman/Jorg & Petra Wegner, p. 8; Bruce Coleman/Stephen Bond, p. 18; Bruce Coleman/Bradley Simmons, p. 22; Farmers Weekly Picture Library, pp. 11, 13, 19; Holt Studios/Richard Anthony, p. 4 (left); Holt Studios/Wayne Hutchinson, pp. 12, 14; Holt Studios/Primrose Peacock, p. 15; Holt Studios/Gordon Roberts, p. 24; Chris Honeywell, p. 25; Images of Nature/FLPA/Tony Hamblin, p. 4 (right); Images of Nature/FLPA/I. Lee Rue, p. 5; Images of Nature/FLPA/Derek A. Robinson, p. 6; Images of Nature/FLPA/Peter Dean, pp. 16, 20; Images of Nature/FLPA/M. J. Thomas, p. 17; Lynn M Stone, pp. 9, 10, 28; Tony Stone Images/Philip H. Coblentz, p. 7; Tony Stone Images/Anthony Cassidy, p. 26; Tony Stone Images/David Woodfall, p. 29.

Cover photograph reproduced with permission of NHPA.

Our thanks to the American Farm Bureau Federation for their comments in the preparation of this book.

Some words are shown in bold, **like this.** You can find out what they mean by looking in the glossary.

Contents

Sheep Relatives

Sheep are farm animals. Sheep are **raised** all over the world. Most sheep are white, but they can also be black or dark brown. Their coats may be long and curly or short and smooth.

There are wild sheep in some parts
of the world. Wild sheep live in the
mountains. Bighorn sheep like this
live wild in the western part of the
United States.

Welcome to the Farm

On a small farm like this, there might be fewer than one hundred sheep. The sheep are kept in fenced **pastures.**

Most of the land on the farm is used for **grazing** the sheep. The rest is used for **crops** of wheat and oats. These are turned into bread or **cereal**.

Meet the Sheep

tail

udder

The female sheep is called a ewe. Ewes can have one or two babies at a time. The babies stay close to their mothers for the first few weeks of life.

eye horn

jaw **hoof**

The male sheep is called a ram. Some rams have horns. They can use them to fight off other rams and **protect** the ewes.

Meet the Baby Sheep

Baby sheep are called lambs. They can walk within minutes of being born. Lambs make a high-sounding noise, called bleating.

When lambs are very young, they
feed on milk from their mother.
Before long, the lambs start to eat
grass and other food.

Where Do Sheep Live?

Most sheep live outside. They are very strong animals. A sheep's thick **fleece** keeps it warm, even when the weather is very cold.

At **lambing time**, most sheep are kept in a barn that has deep straw on the floor. The ewes and the lambs go outside again when the lambs are about three weeks old.

What Do Sheep Eat?

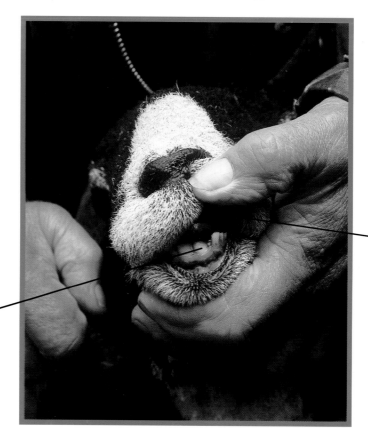

teeth in bottom jaw

pad in top of mouth

Sheep's mouths are made for **grazing** short grass. They bite off grass between their bottom front teeth and upper **pad**, then swallow it. Later they **chew the cud** between their back teeth.

In winter, when the grass stops
growing quickly, sheep eat **hay** and
cereals. They drink water from
troughs all year.

Staying Healthy

Farmers take good care of their sheep. To keep the sheep healthy, farmers make sure they have fresh grass to eat.

Sheep can catch **diseases** and **parasites.** They get them from each other and from the ground. Farmers dip the sheep in a special liquid to kill any parasites.

How Do Sheep Sleep?

As day turns to night, the sheep gather together. They find a **sheltered** area and lie down with their backs to the wind.

Sheep sleep with their eyes closed. If something bothers them, they wake up and run off. They may **graze** for awhile, but they soon lie down again to rest.

Raising Sheep

Farmers sometimes use sheepdogs to help **herd** the sheep. Sheepdogs run around the sheep to keep them together. They can make the sheep move from one field to another.

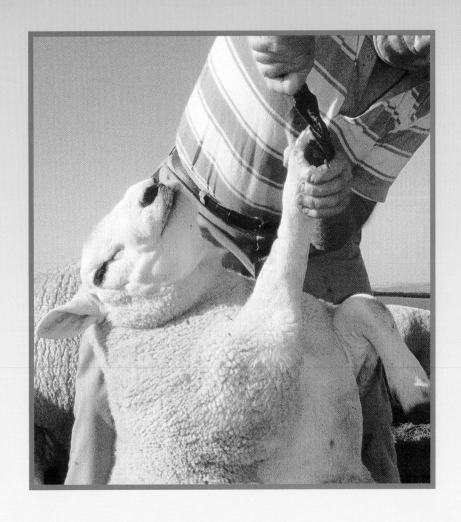

The farmer and his sheepdog round up
the sheep to take care of the whole
flock. Sometimes they trim the sheep's
hooves. This is like cutting your nails.

How Are Sheep Used?

Some farmers **raise** sheep for their meat. The meat from sheep is called lamb.

Lamb can be cooked in different ways.
Roast lamb is a popular food in many
parts of the world.

Other Sheep Farms

Sheep are also **raised** for their **wool.** A sheep's **fleece** is **sheared** off. This is like giving the sheep a haircut. The fleece is sent to a factory to be cleaned and spun into wool.

Some farmers also keep sheep for their creamy milk. They make special cheeses and yogurt from it. There is a special kind of cheese made from ewes' milk called Roquefort.

More Sheep Farms

In some parts of the world, farmers
keep sheep high up in the mountains.
A **shepherd** moves around with the
sheep and takes care of them.

In Australia, large sheep farms are called sheep stations. They have many thousands of sheep. The sheep are left alone for most of the year, until they are rounded up for market.

Fact File

 Sheep prefer being together in a **flock**. If one sheep moves, the others follow it.

 Lambs are born with eight **milk teeth**. Every year, two of their milk teeth fall out and are replaced by adult teeth. After only a few years, these adult teeth start to fall out.

 When a lamb is about one day old, the farmer puts a tight rubber ring on its tail. This makes the tail fall off. It helps to keep the area under the tail clean. It does not hurt the lamb.

Sometimes a farmer needs a ewe to feed a lamb that is not her own. He holds the lamb where the ewe cannot see or smell it. She soon gets used to the new lamb and lets it feed from her.

If this does not work, the farmer's family feeds the lamb from a bottle, just like a baby!

 Australia has more sheep than any other country in the world. In Australia, there are ten sheep for every person.

Glossary

cereal wheat, oats and barley, often made into breakfast food

chew the cud bring food back up into the mouth from the stomach, to chew it again

crop plant that farmers grow in fields

disease sickness

fleece sheep's coat of wool

flock group of sheep that live together

graze to eat grass in a field

hay cut and dried grass

herd to round up animals

hoof (more than one are called hooves) hard pad of a sheep's foot

lambing time time of year when the lambs are born

milk tooth (more than one are called teeth) kind of tooth a lamb has when it is very young

pad hard area in sheep's mouth

parasite little animal that lives on a bigger animal and can make it sick

pasture field of grass for animals to eat

protect keep safe

raise to feed and take care of young animals or children

shear to cut off the fleece of a sheep in one bundle

sheltered safe from bad weather

shepherd person who takes care of sheep

trough food or water container for animals

udder part of an animal's body where milk is stored

wool yarn or cloth used to make warm clothes

More Books to Read

Brady, Peter. *Sheep.* Minneapolis, Minn. Capstone Press, Inc., 1996.

Hansen, Ann L. *Sheep.* Chanhassen, Minn. : ABDO Publishing Company, 1998.

Kallen, Stuart A. *The Farm.* Chanhassen, Minn.: ABDO Publishing Company, 1997.

Index